London Transport in Exile

1950s and 1960s

Kevin McCormack

Front cover: The Guy Specials made excellent staff buses, but comparatively few re-entered stage-carriage service following sale by LT. One that did was GS43, which worked for Southern Motorways and was photographed in April 1969 at Petersfield station in Hampshire. *John Bishop*

Back cover: T. Canham (Services) of Whittlesey, Cambridgeshire, operated two STLs between 1953 and 1960 — STL1739 and STL1836. The latter is depicted at Peterborough bus station. *Harry Luff*

Title page: One of the 12 'Q1' trolleybuses sold to Zaragoza in Spain, LT No 1818, displays its smart livery in 1966. The interior has undergone considerable transformation with the fitting of a central staircase. *Donald Allmey*

Left: Never again to work route 11, 'prewar' RT56 lies derelict at the Royal Earlswood Hospital, Redhill, Surrey, prior to being broken up on site in September 1969. This and sister vehicle RT131 had been acquired in 1960 for patient therapy. *Roy Hobbs*

Right: Sabena, the Belgian national airline, purchased some wartime Guy Arabs for sightseeing duties. This photograph dating from September 1951 shows G35 at Melsbroek Airport, Brussels. *Jack Wyse*

First published 2004

ISBN 0 7110 3021 9

© Kevin McCormack 2004

Published by Ian Allan Publishing

an imprint of Ian Allan Publishing Ltd, Hersham, Surrey KT12 4RG.
Printed by Ian Allan Printing Ltd, Hersham, Surrey KT12 4RG.

Code: 0407/B1

Introduction

We tend to take for granted that, when their working life in the capital is over, former London Transport (LT) vehicles (and those of the successor companies) can turn up anywhere fulfilling a range of roles, including continued passenger service in Britain. But it wasn't always so.

The erstwhile British Transport Commission (BTC) exercised strict control over the sale of buses by nationalised bodies such as LT. Buses could not be used for further stage-carriage service in order to protect other BTC-controlled operators. In the early postwar years this meant that the vast majority of LT's prewar/wartime buses were scrapped, the market for garden sheds, caravans etc being somewhat limited.

Following the end of the tram-replacement programme and with the flood of new RT-family vehicles arriving, LT had to dispose of vast numbers of old buses and did this mostly through dealers. Only one was prepared to take so many — W. North of Leeds. However, the company made acceptance conditional on unrestricted disposal of up to 10% of the vehicles. The BTC was forced to relax its policy, and suddenly STLs and their contemporaries began to appear elsewhere in Britain on bus services.

There had been no such problems for exports and it was fascinating to find, even in the 1960s and early 1970s, a wide range of prewar vehicles in countries far and near. By 2003 all were assumed to have long since vanished and then, lo and behold, a 5T4 was advertised on the Internet as being available in northern France! Within weeks T357, which had been kept safe under cover for over 40 years, was in Cobham Bus Museum in Surrey — a unique survivor and an amazing find, even eclipsing the discovery of T499 in Australia in 1999. It's also quite remarkable that, in terms of early-postwar buses, there are two small fleets of RT-family vehicles still in regular service abroad — six at Davis in California and eight on Prince Edward Island in Canada, all in LT livery.

Harry Luff, an LT Underground driver, took a particular interest in unearthing old London buses, mainly in Britain, claiming that his trusty scooter was fitted with an automatic tracking device! Half of the material in this book is Harry's work, with the remainder being provided by many other photographers — Michael Allen, Donald Allmey, Geoffrey Ashwell, Maurice Bateman, John Bishop, Marcus Eavis, Les Folkard, John Hambley, Mike Harries, Roy Hobbs, Bruce Jenkins, Roger Joanes, Andrew Johnson, Mike Lockyer, Iain MacGregor, Jannes Nijhof, Blake Paterson, D. Trevor Rowe, Ian Stewart, Phil Tatt, Barry Wilkinson and Jack Wyse (the last courtesy of the Light Rail Transit Association, London Area). Grateful thanks go to all those mentioned.

The aim of the book has been to cover LT buses, in unrebodied form, withdrawn before 1970 and put to further use. Routemasters are therefore excluded, and, wherever possible, the earliest material has been used for its rarity value. It is unlikely that such a collection of colour material, gathered from Britain and overseas, has ever appeared before in an album such as this.

A special thankyou must go to two people without whose help this title is unlikely to have appeared in its present form — Roy Hobbs, for his incredible enthusiasm and numerous contacts, and Martin Jenkins from the Online Transport Archive, which is the custodian of many precious photographic collections, including Harry Luff's. As ever, the PSV Circle's fleet histories have been invaluable, as has also been the help given by Maurice Bateman, Michael Dryhurst, John May and Tony Beard in providing additional information. Thanks also to the late Bill Cottrell of Cobham Bus Museum, for making available Donald Allmey's transparencies.

For ease of reference, all vehicles are referred to by their LT fleetnumbers.

Kevin R. McCormack
Ashtead, Surrey
January 2004

Speeding along past the disused Glasgow Corporation tramlines in Renfrew Road, near Paisley North, in 1959 is Cravens-bodied RT1481. This was one of four such vehicles purchased by Cunningham's Bus Service of Paisley. The non-standard Cravens RTs were the most modern buses ever to have reached the second-hand market in such quantity and revitalised many independent fleets. *Ian Stewart*

4

Ayrshire-based A1 Service, an association of independent operators, acquired over 60 RT-family vehicles. Four of them are lined up here in Kilmarnock in 1959, with Cravens RT1429 and RTL44 nearest the camera. The latter was from the first batch of 100 standard RTs and RTLs put up for sale in 1958 as a result of over-ordering by LT. *Ian Stewart*

From a fleet of 131 Leyland Tigers (TDs), 98 were sold to Ceylon (Sri Lanka) and have long since expired. Of those which remained in Britain, four currently survive, including TD130, depicted here in 1964 while owned by Hills Patents of Staines. *Harry Luff*

'Prewar' RT8 stands outside Carson Pirie Scott & Co, a Chicago department store which was promoting a 'British Fortnight' in September/October 1961. Hopefully, this vehicle is still extant, having been sighted in poor condition at an American transport museum during the 1990s. *Harry Luff*

Two unidentified STLs were discovered on the outskirts of
Brussels in the mid-1950s, being used as sheds by a building
contractor. More than 40 of this class were exported to
Belgium in the early 1950s. *Phil Tatt*

The 'Q1' trolleybuses, with the exception of two, were sold to Spain in 1961, and the 125 vehicles in question were dispersed among nine operators. Santander's fleet of six were the most original in appearance, as evidenced by LT No 1812, which has since been repatriated and is preserved at Sandtoft, near Doncaster. *Roy Hobbs*

Left: The 84-strong GS (Guy Special) class was introduced in 1953, some being used to replace the last operational examples of the Leyland Cub C and CR classes. Withdrawal was a drawn-out affair, taking from 1958 to 1972; GS61 was an early sale, to Corvedale Motor Services of Ludlow. *Harry Luff*

Above: Resting in a back garden in Teignmouth, Devon, in October 1960 is LT1059, an AEC Renown which operated from 1931 to 1949 and latterly carried the body of LT1132. Rescued in 1970 and at one time wrapped in netting to prevent further disintegration, the vehicle is now at Cobham Bus Museum awaiting an extensive rebuild. *Les Folkard*

The last STDs were withdrawn from Hendon garage on 14 June 1954, two weeks before the last Central Area STLs. STD50 spent its afterlife with two Scottish independents.

With the outline of its LT fleetname still visible in the sunlight, the vehicle is seen working with Campbells of Fenwick. *Harry Luff*

Outside the Alexander (Midland) garage in Perth on 10 June 1962, Guy Arab G151 stands alongside its replacement, a blue-liveried Bristol FLF, signalling the demise of the red livery used hitherto for Perth city services. *Iain MacGregor*

Despite having its side-mounted engine replaced by a door (the engine must be somewhere else!), as well as extra rear wheels fitted and an extension bolted on the back, this vehicle is still unmistakably a 5Q5. Bearing the fleetname 'CTM' and number 196 (registration CA 17304), it was photographed in Algeciras, Spain, in May 1966. *Les Folkard*

Left: It's Christmas Day 1995 at the Clandestine Immigration & Naval Museum in Haifa, Israel! Standing on blocks (and hopefully surviving the present unrest in the region) is a prize exhibit, ST798, carrying the body of ST30, dating from 1930. ST798 was withdrawn in February 1943 and sold to the Royal Navy, which subsequently converted it into a mobile classroom for submarine-detection training, latterly based at Chatham Dockyard. In 1958 Israel bought some second-hand submarines from the Royal Navy, and the ST came as part of the arms package! *Jannes Nijhof*

Right: LT's first rear-engined buses — 20-seat Leyland Cubs of the CR class — entered service in 1938. All 49 vehicles were stored for much of the war due to their diminutive size and a shortage of spares, and they saw little use afterwards, withdrawal occurring between 1948 and 1953. A few were exported, including these two — CR16 and, nearer the camera, CR36. These vehicles were operated by Lefkaritas of Larnaca, Cyprus, and then left to decay. The remains were subsequently repatriated, and happily CR16 is now in the final stages of restoration. *John Hambley*

It's a tight fit for ex-Maidstone Corporation Guy Arab No 50, STL2377 (now at Cobham) and Cravens RT1514, all belonging to Mulleys Motorways of Ixworth, near Bury St Edmunds. RT1514 is still in the livery of its previous operator, Longlands of Crowland, Lincolnshire, and by the time of its withdrawal in 1975 had become the last Cravens RT in service anywhere. *Harry Luff*

Lloyds of Nuneaton operated factory and school contracts, and among its fleet were Cravens RT1437 and RTL1450, acquired in August 1956 and September 1959 respectively. Both would be scrapped following accidents. *Harry Luff*

The BTC's ban on the sale of LT vehicles for stage-carriage service did not apply to trams; between 1949 and 1951 no fewer than 90 of the classic 'Felthams' from 1931 were sold to Leeds, some lasting until closure of the system in November 1959. On 8 September 1957 LT No 2157 (ex-London United No 388) passes a classmate at the Corn Exchange. *Marcus Eavis*

The 120 RTs bodied by the Cravens Railway Carriage & Wagon Co and delivered between 1948 and 1950 looked nothing like the remainder of the RT fleet and were withdrawn in 1955/6. Demonstrating the curved back of the Cravens body is RT1462, photographed at Garston in June 1964 while in the ownership of H&C Transport.
Harry Luff

Left: Of the 139 standard forward-entrance STLs, five were converted to tree-loppers (of which 971J — ex-STL1470 — survives), but very few resumed passenger service after sale by LT. Here is one, STL1511, which operated until 1960 with R. Whieldon & Sons of Castle Donnington and was fitted with platform doors. *Harry Luff*

Above: Dwarfed by the former Cunard liner *Queen Mary*, Metro-Cammell-bodied RTL564 stands at Long Beach, California, under the watchful eye of Father Christmas. An automatic coin machine has been installed on the vehicle's platform. *Harry Luff*

21

Above: The entire fleet of 65 postwar STDs (Leyland PD1s) was despatched to Yugoslavia in 1955, to be followed in 1956 by an LT bus stop! This example, registered GX2001, was seen on 25 August 1961 in Sarajevo with an ex-Wallasey Leyland PD1 behind; each had had its open rear platform reversed. *D. Trevor Rowe*

Right: This AEC among Leylands is Cravens RT1404 in the striking livery of Barton Transport of Chilwell (near Nottingham), which acquired the vehicle when it bought out Cream Bus Services of Stamford, Lincolnshire, in 1961. *Harry Luff*

Above: Only five of the 15 RFW-class private-hire coaches avoided the one-way journey to Ceylon (Sri Lanka). One of the 'stay at home' brigade was RFW14, seen here at the 'address' of its owner, St Thomas' Hospital, near Waterloo. *Harry Luff*

Right: The last of its class to remain in LT stock, TD118 was loaned to Brunel College, Acton, for a year from November 1963, during which time it journeyed to Moscow. After sale by LT in February 1965 to a group of students who took it on holiday to Turkey (see page 79), TD118 was sold again and became a motor caravan. In this guise it is seen in late 1968 at the Royal Artillery Barracks, Woolwich. *Phil Tatt*

Left: STL1592 and, on its right, STL1614 shared an unusual afterlife with the London County Council Parks Department, being used as stewards' 'cabins' at Crystal Palace racetrack during the late 1950s. *Harry Luff*

Right: The first 31 Leyland PS1 Tigers (TDs), fitted with Weymann bodies and dating from 1946, were all withdrawn by March 1958. TD3 and TD4, shown in 1956 at Birds (dealer) of Stratford-upon-Avon, were destined for Yugoslavia, unlike 24 of the batch, which went to Ceylon. *Phil Tatt*

Left: In the early 1960s LT disposed of its private-hire fleet, consisting of the first 25 RFs and the RFW class (see page 24), all of which had extensive glazing for sightseeing purposes. RF12, depicted here in 1966, spent no less than 17 years operating with Hampson's Luxury Coaches of Oswestry, alongside RF13. *Maurice Bateman*

Above: This Spanish scene dating from May 1961 shows 'Q1' trolleybuses 1775 and 1821 in the process of having new offside entrances/exits fitted and the staircase transposed. The vehicles subsequently became Nos 7 and 6 respectively in the Santander–Astillero fleet. *Les Folkard*

Above: Polyfoto (England) of Watford used STL1815 as a mobile showroom but dispensed with its services in 1958, sending it for scrap. The bus had been one of a batch of 400 roofbox examples introduced in 1936. *Harry Luff*

Right: Sporting a home-made radiator-surround and grille, former Green Line 9T9, T415, dating from 1936, enjoyed the company of another member of this class (see page 57) while operated by Transportes Guanarteme in the Canary Islands. The photograph was taken in March 1963 at Las Palmas. *Andrew Johnson*

Below: Hidden away at Speen, near High Wycombe, since 1950 was the second 'Scooter' to be rescued. LT1076 is now part of London's Transport Collection and likely to be fully restored by the time this book is published. *John Hambley*

Right: In the 1950s and '60s there were several companies in the Watford area using ex-LT vehicles, one of them being Knightswood Coaches. Seen on school contract work at South Oxhey in the summer of 1967 is RT445, with RTL262 behind. *Harry Luff*

A line-up of three 'Q1s' decorates the streets of San Sebastian in a scene from summer 1966 which disproves the theory that the sun always shines in Spain! San Sebastian rivalled Bilbao for the largest fleet of ex-London trolleybuses, each being allocated 25. From left to right are LT Nos 1874, 1854 and 1858.
Donald Allmey

Lying unwanted at dealer North's of Leeds in July 1962 were these two former Green Line coaches, TF30 and TF46. They belonged to a class of 88 underfloor-engined Leylands of somewhat revolutionary design for 1939, the year of their introduction. *John Bishop*

Above: At the age of nine the author thought Cravens RTs looked the same as the rest of the class and could not understand why RT1487, which he frequently saw travelling along Western Avenue, Ealing, painted blue with 'Permutit' written on it, had been sold. Used as a staff bus, it was photographed on the North Circular Road, near the Chiswick flyover. *Harry Luff*

Right: 'Prewar' RT58 looks magnificent at the Stratford-upon-Avon premises of Birds (dealer), having recently been repainted in LT livery, presumably for demonstration or advertising purposes. The vehicle later went to A1 Service but lasted only a short time before being returned to Birds for breaking. *Harry Luff*

This 1948 AEC Regal III, T792, was one of the last four to remain in service as a Country Area bus, not being withdrawn until 1963. It then spent the next three years with Bovis (contractor) as staff transport before being acquired for preservation. *John May collection*

John Stevenson & Sons of Spath, near Uttoxeter, acquired several RT-family vehicles, including Cravens-bodied RT1466, which, typically, has lost its roofbox. The vehicle served the company well from 1957 to 1971, later being fitted with platform doors. *Harry Luff*

Above: Scotland was a popular destination for Cravens RTs, 30 being acquired by Dundee Corporation for tramway replacement (and keeping their roofboxes). RT1520, however, went to Clyde Coast Services and was photographed in Largs in 1963. *Ian Stewart*

Right: Demonstrating that RT-family vehicles did not always re-enter public service, RT3359 and RTW329 passed to Gorray, a clothing manufacturer based in Enfield, North London, for staff transport. The RTW, seen leaving the factory in 1966, is now preserved. *Harry Luff*

Left: Old and new stand together at the premises of Warners of Tewkesbury, an independent still in business today. In the foreground is G336, a wartime-designed Guy Arab from 1945, while behind is postwar RT242 (now preserved), both having been fitted with platform doors. *Harry Luff*

Above: Dodging the Dodges in Malta in the summer of 1967 is Q103, dating from 1936, with bodywork by the Birmingham Railway Carriage & Wagon Co. The vehicle has been personalised by the addition of a bumper (which it did not possess the previous year), some 'go faster' mudguards and a Bedford grille, albeit with AEC correctly written beneath! *Michael Harries*

Above: It is tragic that none of the faithful prewar STD class of Leyland TD4s survives today. STD90, seen here with F. Smith of Long Itchington, Warwickshire, nearly made it; acquired for preservation, it was subsequently badly vandalised and, being deemed beyond redemption, was broken up in 1962. *Harry Luff*

Right: RT54 (now preserved) is seen in the ownership of another Smith, this one based in Reading. The first RTs — surplus 'prewar' buses (actually built during the early part of the 1939-45 war) — were disposed of in December 1955. Smith's turned its examples into impressive-looking vehicles, with platform doors and striking blue-and-orange livery. *Harry Luff*

Above: With rear doors and hoist fitted for wheelchair access, GS70 was put to good use by West Ham County Borough Handicapped Persons' Voluntary Committee in East London. This view dates from the summer of 1967. *Harry Luff*

Right: Premier Travel of Cambridge was well known for its fleet of former private-hire RFs but also acquired other LT types over the years. Here we see STL1697, which ran for six years until its withdrawal in December 1959. *Harry Luff*

Left: Two smart staff buses await the call of duty in October 1964 at Simmons & Hawker's premises at Feltham, Middlesex. Alongside RT4216 stands a 1946 Bristol K6A which used to belong to Crosville. *Harry Luff*

Above: G. W. Osborne & Sons of Tollesbury had only recently acquired former private-hire RF5 when it was photographed in the summer of 1964. The vehicle operated with Osborne's until December 1969 but was scrapped shortly thereafter. *Harry Luff*

Above: The London Brick Company, having attracted a large number of Italian immigrants to the Bedford area in the early postwar years, had to provide transport for them and over a 25-year period operated a total of 60 staff buses. Most were AECs; at the head of their respective lines in this view are 'prewar' RT32 and Cravens RT1499 (now preserved).
Harry Luff

Right: The last STLs in service (apart from the postwar batch) were Country Area buses, withdrawn on 31 August 1954. Like several of the later withdrawals, STL1684 found a buyer, W. Lusty & Sons of London, with which it served as a mobile showroom for six years until its demise in 1961.
Donald Allmey

Left: North's (dealer) purchased all the postwar STLs in 1955, and Grimsby Corporation took six. This photograph from September 1963 depicts STL2694 in the livery of the combined Grimsby-Cleethorpes fleet. This vehicle remained in service until January 1967; the final operational example, STL2692, withdrawn 12 months later, was secured for preservation. *Bruce Jenkins*

Above: One of the first postwar RTs to enter service (in July 1947), RT157 initially joined the fleet of Brown's Blue Coaches following withdrawal by LT and then moved to the northern extremities of Aberdeenshire. Its buyer was Simpsons of Rosehearty, which operated a town service in nearby Fraserborough prior to the absorption of the company by Alexander (Northern). *Maurice Bateman*

Left: Pursued by an ex-Washington DC Transit PCC tram over Sarajevo's recently re-gauged tramway system, a Yugoslavian postwar STD (believed to be STD166) is seen in September 1964 engaged on overhead-line duties (note the heads on the roof!) after conversion to a tower wagon. One STD, believed to be STD171, has been preserved by its operator, GSP of Novi Sad, Serbia, but, when observed in March 1997, had unfortunately been fitted with an unflattering replacement front roof dome. *Blake Paterson*

Above: Gran Canaria's second 9T9, T423, did not suffer the indignity of losing its AEC radiator grille (unlike T415 on page 33), as evidenced by this view of the former coach travelling through Las Palmas in March 1967. Both vehicles lasted into the 1970s, with the result that, despite a London career spanning 1936-54, they probably worked longer in the Canary Islands. *Michael Allen*

57

Left: Now preserved, RTL554 is depicted in the summer of 1967 while in the ownership of an engineering firm based at Harefield, Middlesex. Of a total of 1,631 RTLs, this was one of only 450 to be bodied by Metro-Cammell. Although these bodies were not interchangeable with the Park Royal or Weymann RT/RTL bodies, they were considered to be of superior construction and were not selected for early withdrawal. *Harry Luff*

Above: Photographed in the shadow of Heathrow Airport during summer 1967, lowbridge Weymann-bodied AEC Regent RLH51 was sold to Office Cleaning Services in March 1965 and was originally based in Bristol before moving east. It was withdrawn in September 1968. *Harry Luff*

Above: The diminutive Leyland Cubs of the C class were superseded by the rear-engined CRs (see page 15). Withdrawn by LT as long ago as November 1944, C54 was one of several sold to the Belgian Economic Mission and is seen in the livery of SNCB (Belgian Railways). *Phil Tatt*

Right: Transportes Urbanos del Gran Bilbao took the imaginative step of converting two of its 'Q1' trolleybuses into motor buses. Interesting in having retained its front end despite the addition of an extension, but unlikely to win a beauty contest, this example used to be LT No 1887. *Roy Hobbs*

Passing through Northern France on a summer holiday in August 1967, RTL1050 belonged to Continental Pioneer of Richmond, which was formed by a group of young men inspired by the theme of the Cliff Richard film. Later converted to open-top, the vehicle was subsequently re-roofed by its current owner, David Thrower. The inside of the original roof was apparently autographed by the Beatles following the RTL's proposed use in the film *A Hard Day's Night*, but the scene was cut, and no evidence of their signatures remained by 1967. *Author*

The 120 Cravens RTs were regarded as too non-standard to keep, in view of the surfeit of standard RTs and RTLs. Apart from one which hit a low bridge (the chassis of which now lurks under the body of RT1), all passed to Birds (dealer) between April 1956 and May 1957 and were resold. RT1480 was bought by Wass Bros of Mansfield, which operator was taken over in April 1958 by East Midland, in whose livery the bus appears in this picture. *Harry Luff*

Left: The first standard RTs to be withdrawn following the policy change to sell according to the age of the body rather than that of the chassis were the Park Royal and Weymann roofbox versions. RT551 entered service at Holloway garage in May 1948 and was sold in March 1963 to Sampson Mushrooms of Oving, near Chichester, Sussex. *Harry Luff*

Above: Joining the predominantly AEC fleet of the London Brick Company were two RFs acquired in February 1965. This one is RF190, showing evidence of its Green Line origins on the side of the roof (where the route-board fixings were located). The vehicle went for scrap in 1970. *Harry Luff*

Left: Pulling up behind STL1836 at Peterborough bus station (see back cover) is STL896, owned by another Whittlesey operator, J. R. Morley & Sons. Withdrawn by LT in June 1953, the bus was first used by Longlands (trading as Grey Green Bus) before being sold to Morley's. It was finally withdrawn in December 1960 and scrapped. *Harry Luff*

Right: Between 1959 and 1966 no fewer than 187 RTs, RTLs and RTWs (albeit only four of the last-named) were shipped to South Africa for passenger operation. A few went to East London and Port Elizabeth, but the vast majority were operated by City Tramways of Cape Town, where this photograph was taken. The bus featured here, RTL841, is particularly interesting, because in 1976 it was selected for repainting into LT red to mark the end of London-bus operation in Cape Town in November of that year. The vehicle was subsequently purchased by an hotelier in Matjiesfontein and re-registered; it was still in use in October 2000. *Les Folkard*

Left: One of a batch of 20 vehicles ordered for Midland General but diverted to London, lowbridge RLH12 entered service in July 1950 and was purchased by Elkes Biscuits for staff transport in February 1966. Photographed shortly afterwards at Elkes' Cardiff factory, the bus went for scrap in October 1971. *Maurice Bateman*

Above: Cobham Bus Museum's Guy Arab, G351, was operated by Burton Corporation from November 1953 to January 1967, having originally entered service with LT in February 1946 at Upton Park. It is the only known survivor of London's unrebodied utility buses. *Maurice Bateman*

Left: Displaying imaginative paintwork on its nearside front wing, RTL26 was one of the first RTLs to be withdrawn by LT and was snapped up by Harper Bros of Heath Hayes, Staffordshire, in August 1958. This view shows the vehicle working the Lichfield–Kingstanding service. *Harry Luff*

Above: Sadly, a few vehicles which were the subject of early preservation projects fell by the wayside, often due to storage problems. Q69 served for many years as transport for senior citizens in Gravesend and is seen in subsequent ownership passing Gatwick Airport on the annual Historic Commercial Vehicle run to Brighton in May 1963. *Donald Allmey*

Left: LT possessed only three AEC Reliances, used between 1961 and 1964 to test operation with a separate entrance and exit. All three were then sold to Chesterfield Corporation, with which operator RW1 is seen here. *Harry Luff*

Right: Among LT's wartime utility buses were 281 Daimlers. Upon re-sale to other operators, most of those remaining in Britain were rebodied, but Samuel Ledgard, proprietor of the well-known Leeds independent, kept his largely in original state. In this view D277 leads D234 at the foot of Billams Hill, Otley, in May 1958. Both buses would be scrapped in 1962. *Mike Lockyer*

Right: Platform doors aside, this is what the first 125 SRTs (with new RT bodies mounted on adapted STL chassis) looked like before conversion. STL2525 was one of only six from this 1939 batch which were not transformed into an SRT. Sold by LT in October 1953, it was owned from October 1956 to June 1957 by Graham's Coaches of North Cray, Kent, as seen here. *Geoffrey Ashwell*

Left: Lacking the financial resources to buy new buses in the early 1950s, Yugoslavia had to turn to the second-hand market. Purchases included several LT types — Gs, Ts, LTs ('Scooters'), Qs, STLs and the entire batch of 65 postwar STDs. At a later stage RTLs arrived to replace the earlier generation; this view, recorded on 10 July 1966 in Sarajevo, depicts RTL1060. *Les Folkard*

Above: Spotted in a car park on the A25 near Guildford in the summer of 1967 were RLHs 42 and 43 in their new role as mobile showrooms. The use of lowbridge buses for this purpose was perhaps an unusual choice, given the risk that potential customers might end up with sore heads! RLH43 would leave these shores in 1971, being sold to an American buyer. *John Bishop*

Brown's Blue Coaches of Markfield, Leicestershire, was an early buyer of RTs, but in 1963 the business was sold to Midland Red without the buses, which were dispersed widely; the vehicle shown here, RT420, went to Super Coaches of Upminster. *Harry Luff*

Ceylon had by far the largest fleet of ex-London buses as a result of a Government-backed agreement for LT to provide advice and technical assistance to the Ceylon Transport Board. Between 1958 and 1969 over 1,400 LT buses were exported, consisting of Ts, TDs, RTs, RTLs, RTWs and RFWs. Most of the vehicles had a very hard life in Ceylon, as evidenced by this view of RTW415 in Colombo.
Barry Wilkinson

Above: Leon Motor Services of Finningley, a one-time STL operator, upgraded with RTs. The firm continues in business today and still operates the Doncaster service on which RT155 is seen in this late-1950s view. *Harry Luff*

Right: TD118 crosses Harbour Street in Ephesus, Turkey, on 13 August 1965 on its second European tour, this time carrying a group of Exeter University graduates and their friends. The bus had been purchased from LT in February 1965 and was sold to a scrap merchant in September 1965, following its return from holiday. Surprisingly, it avoided its expected fate (see page 25) and survives today in a Kent barn. *Roger Joanes*